"Like the crash that sets off this book, *Space Junk from the Heavenly Palace* is equal parts mysterious, fiery, and chaotic. From the outermost coastlines of the deep cosmos, to the purple undersides of a dead crab, these poems traverse the borders of race, class, gender, and sexuality to fiercely interrogate a life at the edges. You will laugh, scream, rage. Escamilla has written a book for the comrades and the comadres, for anyone whose ever had get lost to find themselves.'"

EDGAR GOMEZ
author of *High-Risk Homosexual*
(Soft Skull Press, 2022)

"This book beheads bullshit & holds the head up to the crowd with a roar, less as an embattled offering and more an exhibit A-Z of life in occupied territory—occupied not just by colonizers, but also gods, space junk, laundry, love, & toilet paper. Rachelle Linda Escamilla's poems aren't just revolutionary/revolutions, they are formal investigations, lyric experiments, and wrenching excavations of the choked histories just under every so-called 'american' surface."

R/B MERTZ
author of *Burning Butch* (Unnamed Press 2022)

"Love connects us to what is larger than us and to what is larger within us than we thought we could hold. The speaker in Rachelle Escamilla's *Space Junk from the Heavenly* Palace follows that connection where it leads them—emotionally, psychologically, spiritually, politically, erotically—and finds that, in the end, it's all one journey. Unique to each of us. Common to all of Us."

RICHARD JEFFREY NEWMAN
author of *The Silence Of Men*

NOMADIC PRESS

OAKLAND

PHILADELPHIA

XALAPA

WWW.NOMADICPRESS.ORG

MASTHEAD

FOUNDING PUBLISHER
J. K. Fowler

LEAD EDITOR
MK Chavez

ASSOCIATE EDITOR
Michaela Mullin

DESIGN
Jevohn Tyler Newsome

MISSON STATEMENT Through publications, events, and active community participation, Nomadic Press collectively weaves together platforms for intentionally marginalized voices to take their rightful place within the world of the written and spoken word. Through our limited means, we are simply attempting to help right the centuries' old violence and silencing that should never have occurred in the first place and build alliances and community partnerships with others who share a collective vision for a future far better than today.

INVITATIONS Nomadic Press wholeheartedly accepts invitations to read your work during our open reading period every year. To learn more or to extend an invitation, please visit: www.nomadicpress.org/invitations

DISTRIBUTION
Orders by teachers, libraries, trade bookstores, or wholesalers:

Nomadic Press Distribution
orders@nomadicpress.org
(510) 500-5162

Small Press Distribution
spd@spdbooks.org
(510) 524-1668 / (800) 869-7553

This book was made possible by a loving community of chosen family and friends, old and new. For author questions or to book a reading at your bookstore, university/school, or alternative establishment, please send an email to info@nomadicpress.org.

Cover art and author portrait by Arthur Johnstone

Published by Nomadic Press, 1941 Jackson Street, Suite 20, Oakland, CA 94612
First printing, 2023

Library of Congress Cataloging-in-Publication Data

Title: ***Space Junk from the Heavenly Palace***
p. cm.
Summary: As a chunk of the Chinese Space Station, Tiāngōng or 天宫一号 or *Heavenly Palace*, hurls itself into the Monterey Bay, the main character finds themselves enmeshed in the same colorful, chaotic crashing through spheres of space or voids of phones or the dark empty of love and the self.

[1. **POETRY** / Women Authors. 2. **POETRY** / American / Chicana and Latinx. 3. **POETRY** / American / General.]

LIBRARY OF CONGRESS CONTROL NUMBER: 2022947223
ISBN: 978-1-955239-42-4

SPACE JUNK
FROM THE HEAVENLY PALACE

RACHELLE ESCAMILLA

SPACE JUNK
FROM THE HEAVENLY PALACE

RACHELLE ESCAMILLA

NOMADIC PRESS

Oakland · Philadelphia · Xalapa

CONTENTS

introduction

EPILOGUE

reading guide

INTRODUCTION

I remember my mom whispering to *me you don't have to go, mija,* you can just stay here as I cried over my luggage (which was too heavy, and needed to be thinned immediately) on the sidewalk of the departure drop-off at San Jose International Airport. I was about to move to Guangzhou, China for a full-time professor position at Sun Yat-sen University (中山大学) My very good friend had convinced their boss in China that they needed a poet in the English department, and I was given two weeks to decide. At that moment, with my mom whispering in my ear, I recalled the day I flew across the country to go to University of Pittsburgh's MFA program with two suitcases and an appointment to see an apartment that I planned on accepting no matter the condition, because I had nowhere else to stay. I remember saying to myself If I can move to Pittsburgh, I can move to China. My mom's fear and love for me, embedded in that whisper, snapped me out of my crying fit. I stood up, gave her a hug and said well, if I can move to China, I can move to Mars! and the security personnel who watched me break down, helped me jump the line, so I wouldn't miss my plane.

This poetry collection is the closest I will ever get to writing about China. The poems crashed in front of me after my return to the US, while I was watching the Monterey Bay in the darkness of a new moon. I saw what looked like a falling star, then a missile, then a rock, and then a crash into the Pacific in front of me. The changing sight terrified me, I thought I would die, perhaps this was the beginning of some war, or maybe the rest of the sky would follow, but after the crash there was nothing more. I asked my partner what it could have been (they were studying rocket science at the time) they had a quick and definite answer with coordinates: you saw a chunk of the Chinese Space Station, Heavenly Palace (天宫 / Tiāngōng) crash into the Monterey Bay. It was at that moment that I remembered that it was the death of my uncle and my mother's illness that brought me back from China, and that I am so hard grounded in the Central Coast of California, that it doesn't seem possible to leave without the tether of my birthplace.

The other part of the collection that feels particularly relevant is that the first section was all written within the same 6 month period, in the same time, space and place: August 2019 to January 2020; I was working for the Philip Glass Days and Nights Festival and producing Out of Our Minds Poetry Radio show on KKUP Cupertino 91.5 FM driving to Big Sur and San José for work, resting in Monterey for family and obligations and driving to Santa Cruz to visit my lover. The poems were written on my Instagram story feed in moments between, in sleepless nights and restless mornings. The pre-pandemic hustle was in full swing and I was about to launch my first play in New York, and heading to Amsterdam with Philip Glass. I was slated to perform on stage with Iggy Pop, Philip Glass, and Diego Luna at the 2020 Festival. And then the shut down, and the slow dismantling of the organization that put on the festival, the loss of jobs, the shifting of desires, the slipping of contracts and the closing up of all non-essential connections, including my three-syllable lover.

There are no words to describe the quiet empty that comes with an ending of such magnitude: of world travel, of grand opportunities, of the fruits of 15 years of labor in the poetry community, of becoming the full-time, stay-at-home mother that I never really wanted to be, of being cut off from the poly community, of learning to live life at home, of waiting. The publication of this collection is a kind of rebirth, but it skips the dark ages of Covid, it is who I was before my life stopped. I'm not quite sure who I am after this book.

IT ISN'T THAT THE
OCTAGON gets in the way of my body,

it's that you are just far enough away to be something like a planet.

All of my desires are tempered by time   and

elementals like:

laundry

&

deadlines—

all I want to do [ ] [ ] [ ] is drive to you,
silently enter your bedroom
and give you all of my earthly blessings.

My endlessness, my empty.

Our escape into ourselves is revolution.

Our   survival speaks.

I am not a witch or a revolutionary—

I am just a poor, brown woman who found you   amongst the
                                                dying embers
                                                of this moon.

WHEN THE SUN BORE YOU

into being it forgot to tell me—

here I am writhing   sin soaked and begging to be rebuked.

You see,

they punish me bc I see—
they lie and ignore my utterances,

but not you.   My demigod. ||| You see |||

                                        my freshly shaved moon
                                        my ornate planetary objects
                                        my dark matter

This is not a game.
This is the only life we have.

COME WITH ME TO THE RIVER

The body of body
and body of body

and body of water

is like the   space

between us—

time that cannot be held

love

Don't fret   we are just breath— *love*

if you breathe   just breathe   breathe   *love*

if you breathe through the cold

love

it's like the upswing of a syllable

love

sometimes unplanned, but   ever ever   ything.

4

I AM A GALACTIC NOMAD, MY DARLING.

In another life we could have been.

Our house would have been.

We would enter and exit rooms

together   and   not.

Our time

was

greens

and blues

coffers

  with

                                    black tea

                                and Conchas—

But this space time continuum dumped
itself onto us and we have been in chaos.

                    How is it that with you, I'm not in chaos?

There's no undoing the part about time, you know?
It will go, and so will we.

On this sandy memory, I'll always see you:
something like the perfect blue sky through a

wide-leaved ornamental tree.

I THOUGHT TIME WOULD MOVE ME:

                                                      stir this cuerpo

but   even   in the solitude   of this spaceship
                          in the minutiae   of inventory
                          in the empty   of this cargo bay

                          I think of you.

How can you exist when I'm here alone?

All of this ocean between us: sharp as steel

                 glass breakers
                              chromatic swell
                                        no shore
                                        a veces
yeah—yes—sometimes
you are SO bright

I can't tell the difference
between the sky

                                                             and
                              the rows of plastic over dirt
                                             in Salinas.

We are people.

I MADE YOU FOOD. In my culture,

that means I love you enough to give you the work of each mother
throughout time,

you see:

I'm like a sunflower

I come from nothing

from dirt
from desolation and dust

from a dry dry body of earth   but when   I come up

I keep on coming—

I grow in the nothingness that you are
into a top-heavy blossom and
                                    I will give

seed   after   seed
after   seed after
           seed
after   seed

seed   after   seed

after   seed after
        seed
after   seed

         seed   after   seed
             after   seed after
                 seed

after   seed
         seed   after   seed
         after   seed after
     seed

              after   seed

              seed   after   seed
              after   seed after
                 seed
              after   seed

seed   after   seed
after   seed after
     seed
after   seed until

                 you're tired of me

9

SOMEDAY YOU MUST LIVE SLEEPLESS LIKE ME so you can see the

way ocean granite lights up in the early morning moon-

and how do I explain the pattern of the Redwood Sorrel
and their ethereal purple petals?

I live beyond this galaxy.

I cannot walk a path without you on my mind—
without your eyes the same color as the

displaced mud mezclada con micah—
the way my whole self slips into your mouth
like toes in creek dreg.

This breeze is for you   the collapse is coming.

WHY DO YOU ASK ME TO WAIT?

here I wait for   //

crows to peel the sky to nothing //

                                                                then you
                                                                came to being

shaped shadows on

my view screen turned all of the COLORS
                    into other COLORS

Now. You ask me to wait ?||?*Waiting for you is like cleaning the
crystal in a white woman's home.*

Just admit it, SUN, you've not room for me // for my purple lips //
for my tits the color of dirt // for my skin soft and //

sun oh sun sun oh sun, why do you tease me with time?

Who can hide from the sun?   Who can stop stopping
stop

fill me up

                                                                until
                                                                your
 light drips down my leg.

I HAVE NEVER KNOWN THE SUN BEFORE—

I am from the body of a translator   or
My Malinche was a poet who spoke to
Conquistadores Kings   Gods

(that's why they call her a traitor)

But, *My Malinche* spoke to the body of the God with the mouth of the
body of the poet and the language of the self and beyond the self to
make a nation of confused children, like me.

But here,

under the Redwoods of Big Sur—I know who I am not—and some-
times, when I refill the toilet paper in the bathroom for these white
people I remember you.

I have known

painters and teachers, poets and other poets. I've known writers and
readers, bookkeepers, plumbers, waffle makers, maintenance workers,
mushroom scientists, clergy and chefs— I've known parking atten-
dants, bar tenders, bakers, engineers, sailors and soldiers. I've known
web designers, coke slingers, guitarists, directors and producers, cam-
era operators, sound panel repairers, health inspectors, singers, math
teachers and lotto ticket makers I've known comrades and one who
asked me to leave everything for them and live beneath a glacier.

TIME AND TEMPER

Coyote bush and chaparral with sunlight,
soft sagebrush and streams of micah—

> now I know it isn't you, it's me,
> my beaming self.

I would have loved you for a thousand lifetimes,
but I'm back now.

Boots on solid ground.
No more agony w every nothing,

nor wretched desperation over all the
places you said you'd see—

> your golden mouth lies,
> oh but the licking.

And, so, this is what life does:
it dulls the senses

It says   rachelle you are a person, not a fire.
Not a star.

Not an endless   not a
void of pain   and sorrow

                    and struggle
                    and brick walls.

          And you —
                    —you are just a man I could have loved.

With everything a woman like me has—
                    —with voltas, with verbs.

THERE'S AN OAK I'D LIKE TO SHOW YOU—

gnarled branches are my hair
exposed roots to the old dirt road.

I once tried to kiss a man against a
burnt out redwood down the path
from that blue oak.

He taught me pain.

He called it boundaries.

Thankless   silence   engaging only

promises implied without the weight of obligation

plague to my person.

I'm gnarled and falling over like the oak   *I say*

How can I say you are beautiful, but you will lose me   *I say*

because I'm laying   *I say*

                                                            always   *I say*

with my roots exposed   my entangled hair   *I say*

I have no boundaries   no border walls   *I say*

No hang ups about the thoughts of others   no hiding   no
implying   the world is ending   *I say*

Tear down your walls, fucking scum.

I LEFT THE COSMIC COASTLINE and came to form just south of Monterey—

I thought I'd leave the cosmic coastline and come to form,

but I was pulled back by the native thistle

the browning leaves and the pelicans who almost seem communal.

I know once I leave this shore what I face:

Maria Juarez dead at 18 months from a preventable respiratory illness

A baby boy denied a diaper bc Border Patrol said he is too old to have one.

We are ancient: the sun god and the poet
and so we isolate:

come to the river with me //	is sound
this palace where love is sound //	is sound
form with me the rock facing north //	is form
divide hard dirt //	is form
cry at the pebbled shore //	is sound
me in my most natural form //	is form
me in the crook of your arm //	is form

I admit it: I am afraid I love reality //I am afraid, reality.

SOME UNKNOWN TOOK OUR MOVEMENT and broke the

syllogism, ah, but that was bound to happen   i tried to find you
in the city but there was no sky   and when i was in the sky i looked
for you in the skyline   but it doesn't matter   your
you is so sparse now   and the palpitations are slowing   and there
are things like   IDK IDK IDK   that just take you from me
 things that not even my wet pussy in occupied territory   not even
the end of the world can bring you back:

                              no smiles and blinks in rapid succession
                                        no leg and toes
                                     no curated ass shots
                                    or syllables crafted
                                   so carefully for your eyes
                            can draw you from your boundaries,
                          where for enough time i walked a line
                          offering my brown body inside out.

          How do I create time in your heavenly palace?

AND THEN SUDDENLY I'M BACK

Steering wheel | $25 to my name |
a quarter tank of gas |
5 cigarettes until it's time to reload |

I don't know how
I got here or how
long it's been |
but the sun is gone |

Even now | I can feel myself whirring around space and time waiting
for a response that will never come |

My mouth was too full of fire | my body was too empty of your light
|

and I tell myself
Rachelle |||||||||||||||||||| there are other stars whose human form can
take shape in your body |

i plucked you out of the dark sky and made you a god |

| *You didn't ask for that* |

| my body is cold without you |
| I'm growing ferns in the darkness |

| These motherfucking candles are doing nothing |

IN THIS LIGHT ALL THINGS BROWN ARE MORE BEAUTIFUL

as if our   sadness
              beauty   is measured
              by glassy gray skies against chronic ocean.

And the dunes are greener—
and the yellows of the turned fields are more *yellow*

and even the invasive ice plant thick w purloined limbs shimmer in
this morning's blessings.

My sorrow exists in order for me to exist.

My sorrow exists in order for me to exist.

My sorrow exists in order for me to exist.

The barracks with boarded windows are
weathered and will be torn down.

Someday, someone will build new homes over my body and the ghost
of you will only exist in text and sky.

But I loved you for a time,
you burned every synapse.
And my feet hurt,

         but limbs are also memories.

YOU ARE NOT A GOD;
THAT IS TO SAY—

I don't have to burn my body to receive you.

There is no falling bc we do not edge
on the silver of stars or mirror the dark empty of

they who tore me limb from limb and
they for whom all the candles succumb.

I lived in the chaos of that thing gods are good at.
But not you:

I saw the miner's lettuce today and the bush lupine.
I thought I had nothing to give you, but you gave me this poem.

This thing that I thought was dead.
This thing that even the stars couldn't supplicate.

I CANNOT TAKE MY BODY
TO THAT BEACH ANYMORE

The portal from here to there has turned

and I don't want to be trapped   by

                                   by

                                   by

the sun cutting your body

my allness laying silent to preserve   something

                                              something saved.

This world is over.

There is no newness.

The collapse comes.

There aren't enough tins of tuna

or guns to retake the fields

there is no time for love.

So

I rest in shade
grow gills for the afterlife
type my body to words

I am mud beneath
the breath of all that you are

of the hummingbird fucks
of combat devotion

here is my letter,
I'm naked at my computer.

THESE DAYS ARE MARKED BY NOTHING

I can't find my metric feet

oh fuck oh Jesus fuck: I had it all:

>   your pant leg
>   under my palm—
>   your eyes
>   swallowing my nothing—
>   you told me
>   things.
>   You held me
>   there.

This poet writes of stopped time.

>   Of a body that is not mine
>   of loss marked by anger   of
>   anger marked by greed   of the
>   things I try not to be
>   of feet
>   slipping

you left because I left

I left
because I fell
I fell
in fear of you
leaving,
but you never
left
the poet, no.
only
the writer
who lost
their meter.

WE HAVE BECOME NOTHING BUT VIEWSCREENS, SO

the space between our bodies is no longer an anomaly:
your control panel and my control panel are working in tandem, but
these bodiless lights and breathless enumerations are breaking me
down.

<How do we function without the touch of another>

<How can I write poetry during this penultimate chapter>

I do not look for [ ] [ ] [ ] in the archer's belt,
I do not count your name in the syllables of stars.
Now. We are here: I told you we'd be::

bitch on the precipice of granite   <cassandra>

I want irises   twirling vetch   lace lichen

Instead I'm stuck in this form, in the heavenly glow of an engineer's
paycheck.

Please return to me. Risk all that is risked anyway. We can lay under a
fallen cypress and pretend

DON'T DO THIS TO ME AGAIN.

I have already lived alone
on the shore for you

I have already looked for
you in the belt of the archer
[ ] [ ] [ ]

Felt you with nothing to
feel

I've already driven to the
edge

already sat alone waiting
for your anything ANY-
THING

But we know.
Our lives are thrown to
chaos
your kingdom came and
went

You have other bodies to
torture   I have a tenuous
thing

I miss you.

The way I fold in your presence   how all of my interpretations in the
space between

                                     How every time I curse you

you laugh at me

                                   I'm your constant is what

you said

                                   No.

My constants are the moon and her glorious timing.
The displacement of sand with a spring wind.
My constants are miners lettuce and invasive mustard burning hills
yellow.

My constants are the holes in rocks filled with rainwater.

I'm gone.   There's no sunshine

IT IS NOT MY LIGHT THAT BURNS

It is not my light that burns   it's the nonlight they ever
 had
It's the traveling through land that changed hands with babies

huddled in arms   and who knows if they wanted those babies?
It is *not me* who wakes with the morning stars and jumps to work to
expel this endless stream:

> of all bodies of all of the
> bodies of all bodies of all
> bodies bodies of all
> bodies

like mine and not like mine, but mostly the ones whose world is rotten
with obligation.

I cannot empty myself fast enough for all their desires to run through
me.

I don't drive in the wind and follow mountain paths and look for the
center of the universe for me—*haha not for me—for me—*

I escape because they need escape because they called me to this life they couldn't live. The lives they lost crossing the desert or the river or the stagnant lives of a detention center holding cell.

How does a brown body exist in a world of white? Always beneath. Always beneath.

So, morning stars. Coastal granite. Poison oak. I come to you as a vessel of multitudes as absolutely nothing.

I SHARE A BIRTHDAY
WITH FRIDA KAHLO
AND GEORGE W. BUSH

Watery Tyrant
Endless Idiot
Beautiful War Criminal
Sad Leader

The pain in my body lives in the body of my pain and I ebb between
one boundary and another

Reconstructed   stammer
Intense sexual beauty marked by I don't give a fuck.

She loved Diego more than life and fucked Trotsky from my dreams.
He didn't even try.

Sometimes I wake up and think that all I need is you
Then I remember that you have your needs
So I go back

Plank through my body
Kill everybody
Kill everybody
Kill everybody
Kill everybody
Kill everybody
Kill everybody
Kill everybody.

I DREAMED
YOU WERE A POEM

and so text and sky came to me.

Did you know they tore down the old barracks?

But I remember   < all bodies of all of the bodies of all bodies
of all bodies bodies of all bodies >

the dark of your eyes   <of all bodies of all of the bodies of
all bodies of all bodies bodies of all bodies >

our frantic hands in the night <of all bodies of all of the bodies of all
bodies of all bodies bodies of all bodies >

those bodies in a bookstore   <of all bodies of all of the bodies of
all bodies of all bodies bodies of all bodies >

Your thumb inside my mouth before I took stage.
Is the center of the universe reset enough?
I go to lose.
I want to be just a body:
a fuck:
a fight:
a commune:
I want you not. He left me too. She isn't enough. I'm trapped. You
pushed me away, I begged back. I'm a dumb bitch, barracks buried.
Seafoam and the purple underside of a dead crab.

EPILOGUE

MY LEGS AREN'T WORKING, I THINK IT'S TRAUMA

The greatest gift my grandmother ever

                              is that her mother died in
                  childbirth

                              and that she had three
                  infants die
                              of starvation:

one placed in a paper bag
then

handed to her husband in the night by the clinic
Doctor—

bury your first born son in the snow,
in the ice in Texas   *Alejo.*

So when my legs stop working   when the
mud of this mud fills the mouths of   monsters

Give. I say—live, say live.

I WENT TO THE RIVER

I saw the gust blow through the trees and drop the leaves like petals
yeah   like petals.

The river said

    If you just listen to the sounds of the pebbles and
stones

    on top of the red sand
       and
    if you just listen to the tide going out
    you can hear enough music to
    fill your glass and a few others.

She said   *Go find that place where the salt and the fresh water*
mix,   *so I did .*

The river said

    hold on to that blanket with two hands because the
  wind is blowing

   said

You can play in the wind   she
said

But hold on to that blanket!

Put it down when you're done.

Sit and rest mija
Eat something mija
Go home.

COMADRE

be careful w white guys from the South

Lol hes from Portland
remember that time I told you

OMG I had a lucid dream abt u

I got out of being shoved into a van?
Bc I was wearing red Toms lol

                                        ...
                                        ...
                            He was trying to kill

you!

                            Oh yeah. OMG.

I know its crazy.

Do you still have that spirit in your walls?

WE ARE ALL RUINS

We are all ruins   daughter
like
        The jade cove on the coast
        Sandstone
        Sunburned lupine pods
        Molcajetes etched in granite

go go   put the petals you picked on ancestor rock

Pray mamás

Pray

IF I DIE

Divide my daughter between the members of the community

o

Grandma didn't die after 13 pregnancies while diabetic

o

Grandpa wouldn't sign the paper to have her tubes tied

oo

She could have died every time.   She did watch her
babies die:

Body depleted of all things nourishing,
      so

She watered the dirt
so she could smell the
mud.

And maybe   like me
            she'd wish that she
                        could eat

spoonfuls like a lobster bisque from The Clement in Monterey.

TECHBRO ART SHOW IN THE GHETTO

FOR LORNA DEE CERVANTES

This art is empty built atop bones from the barrio that grew
Cervantes —

> The only remnant is in the
> battered, pinewood telephone pole   heavy
> with witness
> and the gutted rice rocket with busted windows and
gas siphoned off.

These unbodied techbros aww at symbols they have never felt:

> the black ink of a Chicano tattoo
> Monarch butterflies   migration

Is this art?
Fountains whose wires are duct taped to the packing shed floor?
White women in headdresses singing hallelujah?

You know
They created this art show to benefit the brown kids
> *But they could have just stayed away.*
Live in suburbia and let the
> the ancestors and descendants grow
> in the cement barrio
> In the plum

Instead. They trample us and exalt our struggles.

                  ask for pity   pick their own pockets
                serve cold IPA in plastic cups

But you know what Lorna Dee?
I could almost see you reading a book by a lamp in a room—
I could almost hear you writing.

LA LLORONA

We used to be wolves   then they blamed Malinche for our

mixed up shit.   I know why she drowned her babies—

who would wish a life in cages?   Of girls who only know

where they are by the designs in the stucco ceilings

                    babies passed around at Disneyland.

Girls face down dead in the desert.

        Daughters living under the bodies of men:

           trapped mothers forced to police skirts:

What did she hear when the she-wolf grabbed her babies and said

I love you, so I will kill you.

                    The sound of a horse
                    The breaking of a branch
                    Was it all in her head?

Who am I to judge the woman who cries for her children by
bodies of water

Tell me what to do?

The rules of my culture are eaten by other cultures and all the cultures
are ruled by men

cry to me   how do I   keep   her   from

drowning?

WE LIVE ON BROWN

AFTER JUNE JORDAN'S "A POEM ABOUT MY RIGHTS"

Here I am tonight, thinking about being a mom and trying to write

this poem about how we can't seem to make enough money without

working our fingers our hands our backs our legs our bodied forms

And that's the point too— that I can't do what I want with my body

because, as June knows, I am the wrong sex the wrong age the

wrong skin the wrong gender identity and whether it's working here

in the would-be halls of education or out there in the celery, it's

never enough.

And suppose it was not just about the working body, suppose I just

want to have enough for my family / I can't' think about it— can't

think about myself thinking about mom thinking about dad, brother cousins, thinking about comrades and comadres and the children /

thinking about the world, all of us —

Even if I just want to get my nails done, and go the beach, write

about the stars and the birds, think about time and the body, meditate

on sex and love and the self, my/self, even if I want to, I could not

because I can't do what I want with my own body—and I'm
reminded of our work and work of our work and work and our

living in silence...

And I can't tell you who set things up like this,

But did you know they can separate our families?

Did you know that they can desecrate the thing that binds us?

And they try, oh they try to profile and deny, they strip and search,

they find new ways to put us in prison, and yet— we still dance.

And we dance even though we are the wrong people of the wrong

skin on the wrong side of their supposed border, and no, I don't

want to be reasonable anymore. Do you get it? We are the wrong people of the wrong skin in the wrong place and the wrong time,

and I know—I KNOW this is what they want me to internalize. But

how can I? I refuse. I refuse.. Because you—you are perpetrators of

Rape and genocide and you want me to reject who I am, where I'm

from and how strong we can be if we choose, for one night, every

night to deny this damned red white and blue bullshit—we deny

your flag, we deny your white and we speak on brown, and we live

on brown.

COULD THE SKY BE ANY COLOR if the word for blue is

The color of my skin in Mandarin is red, brown is absent.

The field full of brassicas is green beneath the missing water
mountains.

       My home is a poem-dry dirt beneath resting bodies: faces
omitted.

Neon orange street signs   dayglo pink hotpants   bodies of
colors walking in malls

      bodies of bodies picking   stories omitted.

Whose bodies enbrowned?
      Skylines beyond too gold hillsides   water omitted.

How do I tell you the color of China, if colors in China are GONE
      the feeling of fuchsia, hard-plastic-blue sandals: a tenuous
rainbow.

Teach a child the star twinkles and it does, tell her it's blue
the sky:

whose omitted story, like the bodies of brown workers, exist.

WE ARE THE
HAPPENSTANCE
OF AN ALGORITHM

determined to be nothing more than a morass of
limbs

we have yet to come undone

vows in front of

California Oak
or   Eucalyptus groves
or a baby who wasn't supposed
to

we   mark time

you are everything nobody else could be

we build freedom with our broken cars   plum wine
we mine for
quarters

when the water jug gets too low

you   fed   her   when I fell apart

you are the color of late
september

you are the color of late
september

TOMB SWEEPING

FOR TIO ARMANDO

I peeled the greasy brown paper off of our bathroom windows in an
afternoon filled with filth.

The construction at the hotel restaurant never stops even for rain or
brake-dust gray skies.

I can't stand this clanging   the men in hard blue plastic sandals carry
thin steel sheets and old men   like children   crowd the work-
space smoking cigarettes   drinking tea.

With Chris's used razor blades I found lips where paper on my win-
dows had lost its hold   So I cleaned.

The process is slow and satisfying except when the paper   brittle
in some areas can't handle the pull and thus splits.

I've dressed like my mother and Tias when they feel the call to clean
something they hadn't noticed needed cleaning before:

> house dress
> bare feet
> bucket full of soap and bleach
> hot hot water
> wedding ring removed

When the gooey paper is removed I can see a new part of the
treetops   across the garden the community umbrella is above
new wooden   western   patio furniture where Chris and I pass
on another glass full of gin and our British friend tells us
stories of the old city: Yemen.

The kitchen looks huge now that the window paper is gone.

the bathroom's exposed from the waist up   the windows are sticky
with adhesive so I have to plunge   hand
                                              after hand into the
                                              bucket   steel
                                              wool against glass
                                              sponge steel sponge
                                              dry dish towel

When the windows are clean I feel accomplished   as if I
discovered a new gurgle of land in the Maldives

I lay in my bed astonished that I've waited almost two years before
noticing the paper blemish.

Now   in the mornings the spring-flowering trees are in
extreme 3D they scream along with the Bulbuls   Chinese
exercise music and construction workers. The white pink flowers
are too many

Too many there are too many

now   too close

I don't remember the flowers being so violent last year   a bush
outside the window is exploding with thin white petals
cartoon-full.

I see the red-flowered cotton tree smiling with life as it drops a
heavy waxy fist-sized blossom   I hear the thud before I see
the heart of the bud burst open.

READING GUIDE

THEME: ABSTRACTIONS OF BODY

Space Junk from the Heavenly Palace begins with "it isn't that the octagon gets in the way of my body," where the speaker of the poem is both implying that this form is obscuring the body, but also that it's not that big of a deal, ("it isn't that") and as the collection continues there are forms of abstractions in the body of the text through typographical features: brackets in place of syllables, white space between phrases, slashes and so on.

DISCUSSION:

- Identify the different bodies in the collection, not traditionally just the body of a person, but perhaps as well a body of water, and so on.

- How do the textual or typographical abstractions function for you as a reader?
  - *What do you think they are doing?*
  - *How are the abstractions pushing on the concept of the body, both literally and actually: in that the abstractions are actually getting in the way of a traditional form?*

ACTIVITY:

- How might you enact textual abstractions with intention to disrupt your own poetic tradition?

THEME: LABOR

My Paternal Grandmother was born in Santa Rita, New Mexico and we are known to be descendants of the Mimbres Apache from the New Mexico region. The Apache people are known historically to be the most resistant to occupying forces, even with the Mexican army altered war currency by paying for scalps and thus contracting the deaths of my ancestors. Santa Rita was also the site for some of the most crucial uprisings in the copper mines against corporations. My Maternal Grandfather was a Bracero; Braceros was part of a labor program intended to break up unions in the west. The California Grower's Association who fabricated a worker shortage in order to justify "scab" labor. My Grandfather fought for basic human rights and testified to Congress about labor conditions for migrants on August 8, 1969. I grew up as a laborer in the orchards during summers, cleaning houses during the school year, and then legal labor when I was old enough. I have held multiple jobs at a time for most of my academic career as well. Labor is a theme that comes up in the collection in many forms.

DISCUSSION:

- In order to move into a collective of resistance, we must alter our collective concepts and refocus our ideas to include words like labor and the laborer. Where is labor apparent in the collection?

- How does viewing love through the lens of labor alter your understanding of love itself?

ACTIVITY:

- In addition to love being labor, there is also a labor of ritual that is involved in the creation and maintenance of art. For example, ofrendas being constructed and supplied by the household, statues dusted, candles tended to. Gloria Anzaldua says that art is an invocation, not just a thing that exists on a wall, it is alive in the body and house of the artist. Meditate on a personal ritual, it could be your cafécito, or the way you wash your face. Write the process. Consider the labor of this ritual; what this ritual is maintaining; who it is invoking; how it looks to write a ritual on a page.

PROMPTS:

- Use an ephemeral social media platform feature (like Instagram Stories) to write lines of poetry that move across time and will disappear in 24 hours. Consider the audience, how they tap forward and back, how long they will look at a page with text. Add stickers and other things that the platform feature allows.

- Envision a character from mythology (in this collection we have Circe, Orion, Malinche, and La Llorona), revisit their story and write yourself into them today. Would Circe order a Vanilla frap? Malinche use DuoLingo?

- Write a poem that enacts falling into chaos.

ACKNOWLEDGMENTS

Thank you to Enca, Chris, Steve, Naomi, R/B, and everyone who has helped me come to shore over the years. Thanks for the poems Homayun.

"Someday you must live sleepless like me" was published by *Monterey County Weekly* during the first week of quarantine, March 2020.

RACHELLE ESCAMILLA

Rachelle Escamilla is a Chicana poet from the Central Coast of California. Rachelle's award winning first book of poetry, *Imaginary Animal* (Willow Books, 2015/ 2022), is now available as a 2nd edition with a foreword written by Chicano poet Manuel Paul López. Escamilla is the founder of a number of creative writing and poetry programs in the US and China; was the producer and host of the longest running poetry radio show in the US; and was a visiting scholar at the Library of Congress, Hispanic Division where her poetry was recorded for Palabra the library's audio archive and her article, *Searching for my Family*, about her grandfather's testimony to Congress in 1969 about the working conditions for migrant workers was published by the Library of Congress. Rachelle teaches Contemporary Chincanx/Latinx poetry and Creative Writing Workshops, manages Social Media and Marketing for *Philip Glass Days* and *Nights Festival* and works as a model and actress.

4 OTHER WAYS TO
SUPPORT NOMADIC PRESS WRITERS

Please consider supporting these funds. You can donate on a one-time or monthly basis from $10–∞. You can also more generally support Nomadic Press by donating to our general fund via nomadicpress. org/donate and by continuing to buy our books.

As always, thank you for your support!

Scan the QR code for more information and/or to donate.

You can also donate at nomadicpress.org/store.

ABOUT THE FUNDS

XALAPA FUND

The Xalapa Fund was started in May of 2022 to help offset the airfare costs of Nomadic Press authors to travel to our new retreat space in Xalapa, Veracruz in Mexico. Funds of up to $350 will be dispersed to any Nomadic Press published author who wishes to travel to Xalapa. The funds are kept in a separate bank account and disbursements are overseen by three (3) Nomadic Press authors and Founding Publisher J. K. Fowler.

Inherent in these movements will be cultural exchanges and Nomadic Press will launch a reading series based out of the bookstore/cafe downstairs from the space in August 2022. This series will feature Xalapa-based writers and musicians as well as open-mic slots and will be live streamed to build out relationships between our communities in Oakland, California, Philadelphia, Pennsylvania, and the greater US (and beyond).

EMERGENCY FUND

Right before Labor Day 2020 (and in response to the effects of COVID), Nomadic Press launched its Emergency Fund, a forever fund meant to support Nomadic Press-published writers who have no income, are unemployed, don't qualify for unemployment, have no healthcare, or are just generally in need of covering unexpected or impactful expenses.

Funds are first come, first serve, and are available as long as there is money in the account, and there is a dignity centered internal application that interested folks submit. Disbursements are made for any amount up to $300. All donations made to this fund are kept in a separate account. The Nomadic Press Emergency Fund (NPEF) account and associated processes (like the application) are overseen by Nomadic Press authors and the group meets every month.

BLACK WRITERS FUND

On Juneteenth (June 19) 2020, Nomadic Press launched the Nomadic Press Black Writers Fund (NPBWF), a forever fund that will be directly built into the fabric of our organization for as long as Nomadic Press exists and puts additional monies directly into the pockets of our Black writers at the end of each year.

Here is how it works: $1 of each book sale goes into the fund. At the end of each year, all Nomadic Press authors have the opportunity to voluntarily donate none, part, or all of their royalties to the fund. Anyone from our larger communities can donate to the fund. This is where you come in! At the end of the year, whatever monies are in the fund will be evenly distributed to all Black Nomadic Press authors that have been published by the date of disbursement (mid-to-late December). The fund (and associated, separate bank account) has an oversight team comprised of four authors (Ayodele Nzinga, Daniel B. Summerhill, Dazié Grego-Sykes, and Odelia Younge) + Nomadic Press Executive Director J. K. Fowler.

PAINTING THE STREETS FUND

The Nomadic Press Painting the Streets Fund was launched in February 2022 to support visual arts programs in Oakland flatlands' schools. Its launch coincided with the release of *Painting the Streets: Oakland Uprising in the Time of Rebellion*. Your donations here will go directly into a separate bank account overseen by J. K. Fowler (Nomadic Press), Elena Serrano (Eastside Arts Alliance), Leslie Lopez (EastSide Arts Alliance), Rachel Wolfe-Goldsmith (BAMP), and Andre Jones (BAMP). In addition, all net proceeds from the sale of *Painting the Streets: Oakland Uprising in the Time of Rebellion* will go into this fund. We will share the fund's impact annually on project partner websites. Here are a few schools that we have already earmarked to receive funds: Ile Omode, Madison High School, McClymonds High School, Roosevelt Middle School, Elmhurst Middle School, Castlemont High School, Urban Promise Academy, West Oakland Middle School, and POC Homeschoolers of Oakland.